THE LITTLE BOOK
ELEPHANTS

Christine Harris
Illustrated by Terry Denton

Hodder
Children's
Books
Australia

FOR THeLMa aND RON BOLaND,
WHO HaVe 300 eLePHaNTS.

A Hodder Children's Book

Published in Australia and New Zealand in 2000
by Hodder Headline Australia Pty Limited,
(A member of the Hodder Headline Group)
Level 22, 201 Kent Street, Sydney NSW 2000
Website: www.hha.com.au

National Library of Australia Cataloguing-in-Publication data

Harris, Christine, 1955- .
The little book of elephants.

ISBN 0 7336 1172 9.

1. Elephants – Juvenile literature. 2. Wit and humour, Juvenile.
I. Denton, Terry, 1950- . II. Title.

599.670207

Designed by MATHEMATICS
Printed in Australia by Griffin Press, Adelaide.

THE Greek WORD eLePHaS meaNS 'iVORY'.

HEARD THIS ONE?

Elephants can hear other animals from a distance of three kilometres.

Their ears have a network of blood vessels which give off heat.

To release excess heat,

elephants flap their ears. The hotter it is, the more they flap. If an elephant is confident, but wants to frighten away another animal, it will TRUMPET loudly, SHAKE its head and CRACK its ears like a whip against its body.

It might also bluff the other animal by pretending it is going to charge. If the charge is for real, the elephant will curl up its trunk and run straight at its enemy.

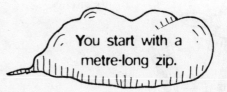

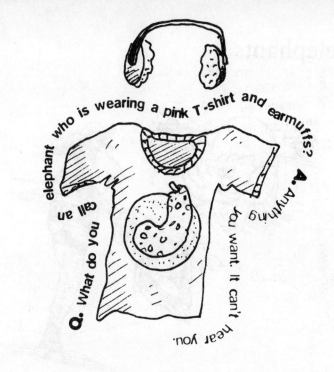

Q. What do you call an elephant who is wearing a pink T-shirt and earmuffs? A. Anything you want. It can't hear you.

Male elephants

are called bulls.

Females are cows,

while baby elephants are calves.

What game
do elephants
like to play?

Squash.

WHAT'LL YOU HAVE?

Elephants are fond of beer
and other kinds of alcohol.

They sometimes eat fermenting fruit,
which makes them drunk.

What did the elephant say
when it walked into the bar?

OUCH.

HE'S GOT THE HIDE
OF AN ELEPHANT

An elephant's skin is two to four centimetres thick. It is almost hairless, with just a few bristles around the ears, eyes, mouth and at the tip of the tail. Despite its thickness, the skin is tender, and mosquitoes, flies, and other insects can easily bite it.

Elephants do not have sweat or grease glands. To keep their skin in good condition, they bathe regularly and wallow in mud, protecting themselves from the hot sun and insect bites. Rubbing their skin with grit and sand removes old skin.

DUCK!

What do you give a seasick elephant?

LOTS OF ROOM.

Why are elephants Big, grey & WriNkled?

Because if they were small, white and round, they'd be Disprin.

What do elephants take if they are hysterical?

Trunkquilisers.

AFRICAN ELEPHANTS

African elephants live south of the Sahara. Their ears are similar in shape to a map of Africa, and can be as wide as 1.2 metres and cover the elephant's shoulders.

Their skin is darker and more wrinkled than that of Asian elephants. African elephants are bigger and have larger tusks. They are tallest at the shoulders and have flat, sloping foreheads, and two finger-like extensions at the tip of their trunks.

ASIAN ELEPHANTS

sian elephants live in parts of India and South-East Asia. Their ears resemble a map of India. They are shorter and wider than African elephants, but have larger toenails and thicker trunks. Asian male elephants (or bulls) have small tusks, and the females (or cows) only have tusk-like teeth called 'tushes'.

BIG TOE NAILS

The back of an Asian elephant curves up in the middle, and its forehead has two prominent bumps. Its skin is light grey, but may have pink or white freckles. There is only one extension on the tip of its trunk.

How can
you tell if
there is an
elephant
under
your bed?

Your
head is
touching
the ceiling.

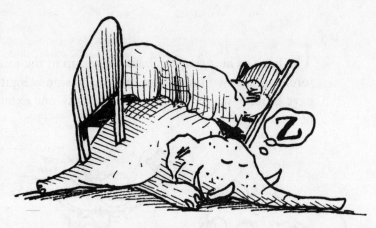

Why can't an elephant ride a bicycle?

Because it doesn't have thumbs to ring the bell.

WHY ARE ELEPHANTS WRINKLED?

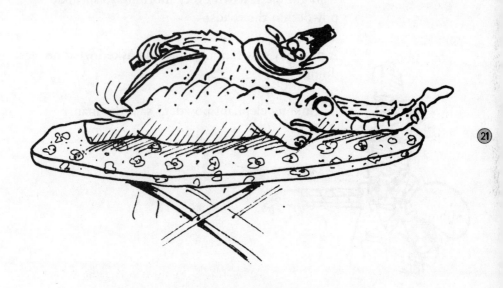

Ever Tried iRoNiNG oNe?

There was a man

who got up at dawn every morning to sprinkle powder on the roads.

A passerby saw him one day and asked what he was doing.

'Sprinkling elephant powder,' said the man.

The passerby shook his head. 'But everyone knows there are no elephants in Australia.'

The man smiled. 'It must be working then.'

A BIRD IN THE HAND IS WORTH TWO IN THE BUSH

Birds, such as egrets, often hang around elephants and sometimes ride on their backs. These birds eat insects that are stirred up as the elephants move. If the birds are frightened away, the elephants know to watch out for danger.

WHY DO ELEPHANTS **LIE** ON THEIR **BACKS** WITH THEIR **FEET** IN THE **AIR?**

TO TRIP BIRDS.

GOOD LUCK

Elephant charms are considered to bring good luck in many countries. In past times, women from the East made tea from elephant dung during pregnancy.

Ganesha, the elephant-headed son of Shiva and Parvati (Indian gods), is worshipped by Hindus as an opener of the way, compassion and good luck. His large elephant ears are believed to help him select the honest words when humans speak. Ganesha's best-known symbol is the swastika.

An elephant's brain weighs five kilograms.

FIVE KILOGRAMS OF FAT, MORE LIKELY

27

WANT TO MAKE A TRUNK CALL?

The trunk of an elephant has over 140,000 muscles.
An adult trunk can grow to two metres long and weighs
around 140 kilograms.

Trunks help elephants...

breathe   smell   feed   drink   scratch   throw things
explore   shower   pick up objects   caress   make noises

Elephants also use their trunks as snorkels, so they
can breathe when they are submerged in water.

An elephant's trunk can:

Suck six to eight litres of water at the one time,

Carry a log weighing up to 270 kilograms,

Pick up an object as small as a coin,

Smell humans over one kilometre away!

IF AN ELEPHANT IS UPSET, IT WILL BANG ITS TRUNK ON THE GROUND.

When they first meet,

elephants touch each other's faces to sniff the scent produced by their glands. They do this by placing the tip of their trunk in the other elephant's mouth.

Young bull elephants play-fight by wrestling with their trunks. It takes a year for a calf to control its trunk.

Mothers comfort their calves by stroking them with their trunks.

If an elephant's trunk is badly damaged, the elephant will die because it can't eat or drink.

AARHH!

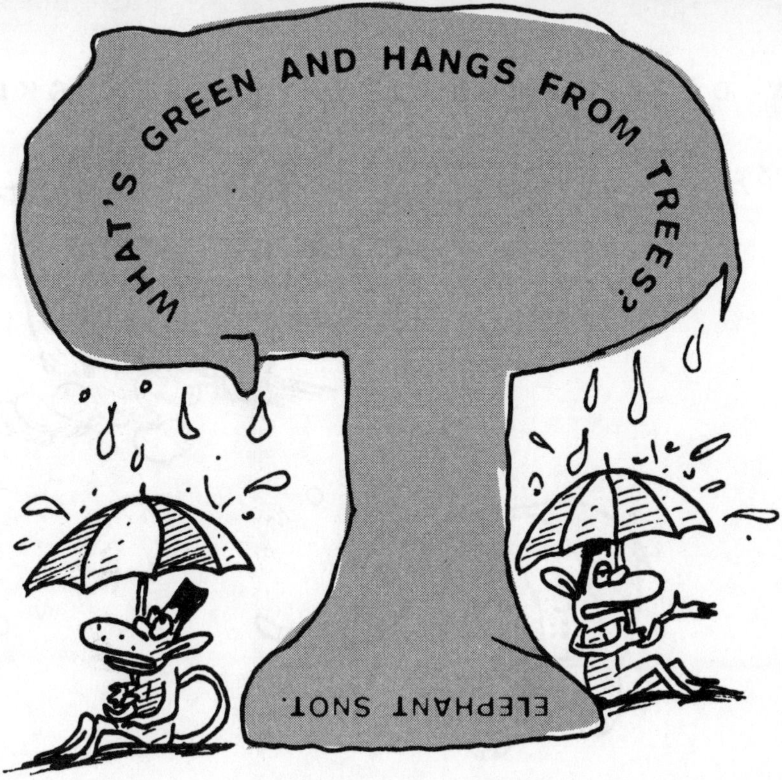
WHAT'S GREEN AND HANGS FROM TREES?
ELEPHANT SNOT.

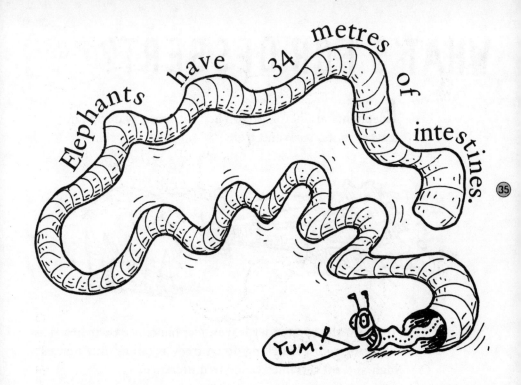

WHAT'S FOR DESSERT?

Elephants are herbivores. They eat grass, water plants, leaves, roots, bark and fruit.

To reach the top tender leaves, elephants use their heads as battering rams, knocking down trees as tall as nine metres high and 60 centimetres in circumference.

An adult elephant eats for 16 hours each day,
swallowing about 2,000 mouthfuls.

CHOMP!
CHOMP!
CHOMP!
CHOMP!

Depending on its size, it consumes 150–250 kilograms daily,
and drinks up to 150 litres of water.

In captivity,

elephants only eat half the amount they do in the wild because the food has more nourishment. They can live without water for three days, and will travel as far as 80 kilometres to find it.

Calves begin to eat grass

when they are three to four months old, and need their own mother's milk until they are two years old. However, they often continue to be nursed for up to five years. Calves drink 9.5 litres of their mother's milk every day.

What do an elephant and a plum have in common?

They are both purple, except for the elephant.

What did Jane say when she saw the elephants?

'Here come the plums.' (She was colour blind.)

HELP!

Elephants are easily frightened. A gunshot can cause an entire herd to panic.

Many years ago, at the London Zoo, an elephant dropped dead with fright during a thunderstorm.

Another elephant caused a stampede because a mouse frightened it.

If the females and calves of a herd are threatened, and there are males nearby, the male elephants will protect them. Females will stand in a circle, with the calves in the middle.

WHAT KIND OF ELEPHANTS LIVE AT THE NORTH POLE?
COLD ONES.

THERE'S NO-ONE ELSE LIKE ME

Every elephant has its own personality
and can remember things for a long time.

JUMBO TRIVIA NIGHT

In 1903, a zoo elephant called Jingo was sent across the Atlantic in a ship. It was so attached to its London keeper, that it refused to eat from the moment it was separated from him.

Jingo died at sea.

JINGO

JINGO

HIS TRUNK.

WhAT dO yOu GeT wHeN you crOsS aN ELEPHANT with a KANGAROO?

Huge holes in your backyard.

46

Why did the elephant go to the beach?
To check out the latest style in trunks.

What happens when an elephant jumps into a pool?
It gets wet.

THINK I'VE PUT ON WEIGHT?

Elephants are the largest living land animal
and
the
second
tallest
(a giraffe is taller).

African bull elephants can grow to a height of four metres,
and weigh 5,000–7,000 kilograms.

Asian bull elephants can reach a height of three metres,
and weigh up to 3,000 kilograms.

In the wild,

elephants live for about 60 years. Some captive elephants live longer.

When an elephant is dying,

it moves away from its herd.

Elephants have a strong reaction to the bones of a dead elephant. They smell the bones, play with them, and scatter them.

Some experts suggest this is because the elephants are trying to recognise whose bones they have discovered.

Other people wonder if the elephants are remembering the one who has died, and are grieving.

WHY DID THE ELEPHANT FALL OUT OF THE TREE?
IT WAS DEAD.

WHY DID THE SECOND ELEPHANT FALL OUT OF THE TREE?
IT WAS GLUED TO
THE FIRST ONE.

WHY DID THE THIRD ELEPHANT FALL OUT OF THE TREE?
IT THOUGHT IT WAS A GAME.

WHY DID THE TREE FALL OVER?
IT THOUGHT IT WAS AN ELEPHANT.

I'LL HAVE A JUMBO, PLEASE

DURING THE 1800S AN African elephant called Jumbo became famous.

HE LIVED IN THE LONDON Zoo for 17 years and visitors came from all over the world to see him. He stood 3.4 metres tall and weighed more than 6,500 kilograms.

THE LONDON ZOOLOGICAL Society became afraid that Jumbo might become a danger because of his size. In 1882, he was sold to the United States showman, P.T. Barnum, for US$10,000. The English public was sad to see Jumbo leave their country, and protested. But Jumbo was loaded on board a ship and taken across the Atlantic to New York. Thousands of Americans turned out to see him arrive. Jumbo became the star attraction of Barnum's circus.

IN 1885, JUMBO WAS KILLED by a freight train. Some say he became angry and head-butted a railway carriage. Others say he was simply standing on the track, caught between a line of circus cars, or that he was trying to protect a younger elephant.

P.T. BARNUM HAD JUMBO'S hide cleaned and stretched over a wooden model at Tufts University. The hide weighed almost 700 kilograms. Jumbo's skeleton, consisting of more than 2,000 bones, was donated to the American Museum of Natural History in New York.

NOW, 'JUMBO' HAS BECOME A common adjective for anything that is really large.

Hi.

ONE AND ONE
EQUALS THREE

Cow elephants mate for the first time when they are 11 years old. Bulls mate at an older age, when they are big enough to fight off rival males.

A cow elephant is pregnant for 22 months and gives birth every four or five years. When she is about to give birth, she moves away from the herd. Another female, usually an experienced relative, goes with her.

An African elephant calf, when it is born, weighs about 115–145 kilograms and is almost one metre tall. An Asian calf weighs 100 kilograms and is 85 centimetres tall.

WHAT DO YOU
GET WHEN YOU CROSS
AN ELEPHANT WITH A WHALE?

A SUBMARINE WITH A SNORKEL.

How do you fit an elephant into a matchbox?
By taking out the matches first.

MOTHER KNOWS BEST

Female elephants live in herds of other, closely related, females. A herd usually consists of 15–30 females and their calves, sometimes more.

Elephants are always on the move. They travel in search of food, water and shade. They are matriarchal, which means they have a ruling female. The head female knows the migratory routes, where to find trees for fruit, and water in droughts. This knowledge is passed on to younger females.

Bull elephants stay separate to the females most of the time, unless there is danger to the herd or they want to mate. They travel either in small male groups or alone. Old males live alone.

An elephant calf always stays near its mother. If it is frightened, it hides between its mother's front legs. Calves sometimes suck on the end of their trunk, just like human babies suck their thumbs. Female calves stay with their mother till she dies, while males leave the herd at 14 years of age.

When a young bull becomes too big or rough in his play, the females bump into him, hard, until he leaves the herd. This is to protect the smaller calves.

HE DIDN'T PUT A FOOT WRONG

There is a pad of tissue on the sole of an elephant's foot that acts as a cushion. The foot expands with the animal's weight, then contracts when it lifts its leg. Because its feet are smaller when lifted, an elephant can easily pull its legs free when it sinks deep into mud. This foot tissue also absorbs the shock of impact. Therefore, despite its weight, an elephant can walk almost silently.

Elephants walk at five to 10 kilometres an hour. On long journeys, they do six kilometres every hour and, although they can't sustain the speed for long, they charge at 40 kilometres an hour when frightened or angry.

Because one foot always remains on the ground, elephants never run, only walk (even at 40 kilometres per hour). They can't gallop or jump, but they can swim for long distances.

WhY DiD tHE eLePHANT cross the road?

Because it was handcuffed to the chicken.

An elephant's molar can be 30 centimetres long (about the length of a house brick), and weigh four kilograms.

ELEPHANT TOOTH FAIRY.

Why did the elephant wear white tennis shoes?
Its green ones were in the wash.

How do you get down from an elephant?
You don't. You get down from a duck.

How do you know that there are two elephants in your fridge?
The door won't close.

WHAT HAVE YOU GOT FOR ME?

White albino elephants have been considered sacred in Thailand and other Asian countries. Being rare, these elephants cost a lot to keep. They could not be used for labour, required special foods, and the owner had to keep up a service for people to come and worship. He couldn't kill the white elephant, or sell it.

o o

ALBINO ELEPHANT IN THE SNOW

If the King was annoyed at someone, he would send a white elephant as a gift. It seemed polite, but it often led to financial ruin. A white elephant was a gift you sent to someone you wanted to destroy.

HOW MANY MOVES DOES **IT TAKE TO** PUT AN **ELEPHANT** IN THE **FRIDGE?**

THREE. YOU OPEN THE FRIDGE, PUT IN THE ELEPHANT, THEN CLOSE THE DOOR.

SALT OF THE EARTH

Like all animals, elephants need salt and they know instinctively when they need it. When elephants are hungry for salt, they dig at soil or rocks with their tusks to taste it. One elephant can eat up to 25 kilograms of salt in an hour.

On Mount Elgon, on the border between Kenya and Uganda, there is a cave called 'Kitum'. It stretches 160 metres into the mountain, is four metres high and 40 metres wide at the entrance, widening to 100 metres inside. Some scientists believe this cave may have been formed by generations of elephants mining for salt.

MAD ABOUT YOU

'Musth' is a time when Asian and African bull elephants go wild. A gland between the eye and ear produces an oily substance and the elephant becomes excitable and dangerous. It happens to males more often than females.

During Musth, for a short time, a bull elephant might rush around, challenging every male he finds—even bigger and stronger ones. He will be keen to mate. As bull elephants grow older, Musth lasts longer. A 30–40-year-old bull will be in this state for two to three months at a time.

WHAT DO YOU KNOW
WHEN YOU SEE THREE
ELEPHANTS WALKING
DOWN THE STREET
WEARING RED T-SHIRTS?

They belong to the
SAME TEAM.

Elephants have bad eyesight.

LOOK, MUM, NO HANDS!

Elephants are important. They...

open up densely wooded areas by feeding on trees and other plants, so more animals can live in these open habitats;

dig up dry riverbeds to reach water beneath the surface, so other animals can also drink;

create paths when they travel, and these can be used by animals such as antelopes and zebras;

fell trees that make good food for small animals;

spread seeds in their dung (some seeds grow better if they pass through an elephant's gut).

DID YOU HEAR
ABOUT THE
ELEPHANT
THAT HAD
DIARRHOEA?

(80)

IT WAS ALL OVER TOWN.

What is the difference between African and Asian elephants?

About 5,000 kilometres.

How does an elephant get down from a tree?

It sits on a leaf and waits for autumn.

KNOW WHAT I'M SAYING?

Elephants are intelligent.

Studies have shown there are at least 25 different calls elephants use, and each has a specific meaning. Among others, they trumpet, squeal, roar and gurgle.

Loud trumpeting helps them locate each other. They also use low rumblings (sometimes called 'infrasound'), which travel for kilometres but cannot be heard by humans.

Elephants also use visual signals.

They move their trunk or ears to get messages across.

Then there is their sense of smell.

A bull elephant can tell if a cow is ready to mate by her smell, and a cow can recognise her calf this way, too.

MUMMY, MUMMY, HE DIDN'T HAVE TO DRILL!

An elephant has six sets of teeth during its lifetime. The old teeth are progressively replaced by the new, which grow, in turn, from the back of the jaw.

Teeth are important because elephants grind their food, and if an elephant can no longer chew, it starves. Old elephants with worn teeth often live in swamps where the vegetation is soft and easy to digest.

Why did they throw the elephants out of the swimming pool?

They couldn't hold up their trunks.

**WHAT WAS THE
ELEPHANT DOING
CROSSING THE ROAD?**

ABOUT SIX
KILOMETRES AN HOUR.

DON'T WAKE ME EARLY

Elephants only need a few hours sleep, usually in the early hours of the morning. They sleep standing up or lying down on their sides. Sometimes they use vegetation as a pillow.

Some elephant trainers sleep near their animals. The elephants, when they are ready to sleep, feel around with their trunks to work out where their trainer is before they lie down, so they don't squash him.

ELEPHANTS OFTEN SNORE.

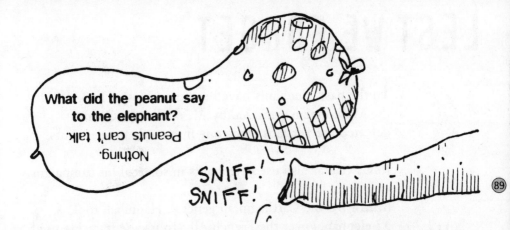

What did the peanut say
to the elephant?

Nothing.
Peanuts can't talk.

SNIFF!
SNIFF!

WHY DO ELEPHANTS
WEAR SNEAKERS WHEN
BOUNCING FROM TREE TO TREE?

SO THEY DON'T
WAKE UP THE NEIGHBOURS.

LEST WE FORGET

In the past, elephants have been used in war. In 331 BC the Macedonian army, led by Alexander the Great, defeated the Persians who rode into battle on elephants.

Julius Caesar also used elephants in some of his campaigns.

In 218 BC the Carthaginian general, Hannibal, took 37 elephants over the French Alps to invade Italy. He used them to shatter enemy lines, in the same way we use modern-day tanks. Sadly, only one elephant survived until the victory parade.

What do you call two elephants on a bicycle?

Optimistic.

POINT THAT OUT FOR ME

TOO MANY CRUSTS.!!

An elephant's tusks are used as weapons, and as tools for digging and levering logs. They grow continuously during an elephant's lifetime—as much as 18 centimetres a year.

African elephants can have tusks that are three metres long and that weigh 25–80 kilograms. The tusks of Asian elephants grow to two metres long. Calves grow 'milk tusks' which fall out before they are two years old, and are then replaced by permanent tusks.

Tusks are made of ivory. They are mostly solid, except for the hollow root which fits into the face bones. A nerve runs into the tusks, so if poachers cut them out while the animal is still alive, the elephant has a painful death.

WHO'S THERE?

Elephants have only a few enemies: lions, crocodiles, snakes and, their greatest threat, humans. If lions or hyenas are hovering, the head female will chase them away. Usually it is calves or dying elephants that are taken by packs of meat-eating animals or large crocodiles. Because of their size, however, elephants are not usually threatened by any other animals.

STOMP!

What is grey, beautiful, and wears glass slippers?

Cinderelephant.

Why did the elephants wear sunglasses?
They didn't want to be recognised.

What do you do if an elephant sits in front of you at a movie theatre?
Move.

(94)

What did Tarzan say when he saw the elephants?
Nothing. He didn't recognise them because they were wearing sunglasses.

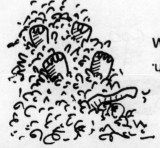

Why do elephants paint their toenails red?
So they can hide in the strawberry patch.

HUMANS

Elephants are used in religious and cultural ceremonies in many Asian countries and are kept in zoos or circuses.

Some say that if elephant numbers keep decreasing in the wild, captive elephants may be vital to the species' survival.

Others are concerned that elephants are slow to settle in a new environment or among strange elephants, and shy about mating in captivity. These people feel it is unkind to keep them, often alone, in a small enclosure away from their family herd.

Although both African and Asian elephants can be trained to work for humans, it is usually Asian elephants that are used for this. For thousands of years, Asian elephants have carried kings, pulled carts and hauled timber from forests.

Some people insist that elephant training can be cruel, and that the animals are made to work long hours and then sometimes abandoned because they are too old or weak to work.

On the other hand, men who work in the jungle with elephants say the animals can work cheaply. They don't need petrol (just plants) and this reduces both expense and air pollution. Furthermore, elephants always instinctively know the shortest and quickest way back to the logpile, making work faster and more efficient. Elephants can manage rough terrain where it would be impossible for machinery to get through and, because of the special padding on their feet, there is little damage to the forest floor.

Many handlers claim to have special and affectionate relationships with their elephants and say they look after them and have no wish to hurt them.

FOLLOW THE LEADER

Training elephants is not easy, as they have complex emotions and different personalities.

In the past, training methods have not always been kind. Some trainers beat elephants with sharp instruments to break their will. Others, seated on trained elephants, drove wild ones cross-country to stockades. There, they were roped between two tamed elephants.

To train them, men would keep the wild elephants awake for two or three nights by singing and lighting fires. They did not feed them and, after a few days, the elephants were so tired and hungry that they finally allowed the men to touch them and to ride on their backs.

WHY DO ELEPHANTS WEAR SANDALS?

TO STOP THEM FROM SINKING IN THE SAND.

WHY DO OSTRICHES BURY THEIR HEADS IN THE SAND?

TO LOOK FOR ELEPHANTS THAT DIDN'T WEAR SANDALS.

DANGER

Serious danger to elephants came in the late 1800s when British planters in India established tea plantations. To protect the tea plants, many elephants were shot or captured.

Poachers in Africa, seeking precious ivory, used to catch elephants by digging deep pits, and covering them with sticks or grass so the animals would fall in. Today, they shoot them with high-powered automatic rifles, sometimes from helicopters.

Between 1979 and 1989, when ivory reached a price of US$200 a kilogram, the elephant population was halved. Up to 300 were killed every day and elephants were in danger of being wiped out.

WHERE IS EVERYONE?

Elephant numbers have been drastically reduced because...

they have been killed for their ivory tusks; and

they have lost a lot of habitat (their natural home). People settled on land where elephants lived; farming and industry threatened natural resources needed by elephants to survive; and the forest has become smaller and deserts are getting bigger

WHERE DO I PARK?

To protect them, many elephants have been placed in national parks and reserves. But when they are squeezed into small areas and their numbers increase, there is often not enough food. Elephants can destroy trees faster than they can grow.

When elephants try to leave the park, they are shot for raiding farms. If they stay, the park warden has to decide whether to kill some of the elephants or let them die slowly of starvation.

It is a challenge to learn how to protect elephants and preserve enough habitat for the natural balance to return.

In 1989 the Convention on International Trade in Endangered Species of Wild Fauna and Flora (CITES), administered by the United Nations, banned all trade in ivory and other elephant products.

Why do elephants wear green tennis shoes?

So they can hide in the grass.

WANT TO BE FRIENDS WITH AN ELEPHANT?

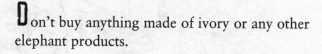

Don't buy anything made of ivory or any other elephant products.

If you already own something that is made of ivory, don't wear or display it.

If you find a shop or stall that is selling elephant body products (there are still some in various countries), tell the owners that you will not use that store again until these products are removed.

Ask conservation groups about clubs or organisations that support elephants.

Ask the local zoo if they are involved in any overseas elephant conservation projects.

Send letters to the editors of local newspapers describing the plight of the elephant and how we can all help in their survival.

WHAT DID TARZAN SAY WHEN HE SAW THE ELEPHANTS?

'LOOK, HERE COME THE ELEPHANTS!'

ELEPHANT WEBSITES

If you want to know more about elephants or see some cool photographs, check out these websites. (Keep in mind that website addresses sometimes change.)

WORLD WILDLIFE FUND (or The World Wide Fund for Nature)

http://www.panda.org/resources/factsheets/species/frame.htm?33eleph.htm

IVORY HAVEN
http://www.geocities.com/RainForest/2248/

ADDO ELEPHANT NATIONAL PARK IN SOUTH AFRICA (photographs)
http://www.jan.ne.jp/~kawabe/addo/

THE WILDLIFE PRESERVATION TRUST INTERNATIONAL
http://www.thewildones.org/Animals/elephant.html

AFRICAN ELEPHANT CONS
http://www.lab.fws.gov/lab/c

DISCOVERY CHANNEL SCHOOL (elephant fact crossword)
http://discoveryschool.com/specials/aek/fun.html

POTOMAC MUSEUM GROUP (elephant skeletons)
http://natural-history.com/modules.html

**LIVING WITH ELEPHANTS (Field Notebook of Iain
Douglas-Hamilton, founder of Save the Elephants in
Africa—photographs and information)**
http://eagle.online.discovery.com/area/nature/elephants/elephants.html

ELEPHANT SATELLITE TRACKING IN MALAYSIA
http://www.si.edu/elephant/

ELEPHANT SCIENCE, HISTORY & EDUCATION LINKS
http://wildheart.com/wwwlinks/main_links.html#213

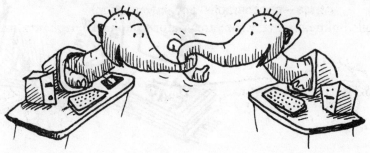